SURVIVING DIVORCE:

Strategies For Before And During Your Divorce To Thrive In Your New Life

Susan K. Duke, Esq.

Jacobs & Whitehall
73-03 Bell Blvd, #10
Oakland Gardens, NY 11364
(888) 570-7338
www.jacobsandwhitehall.com

Ordering Information:

Quantity sales. Special discounts are available on quantity purchases by corporations, associations, and others. For details, contact the publisher at the address above.

Orders by U.S. trade bookstores and wholesalers. Please contact Jacobs & Whitehall: Tel: (888) 991-2766 or visit www.jacobsandwhitehall.com.

Printed in the United States of America

Published in 2021

ISBN: 978-1-951149-83-3

Preface

This book is not meant to encourage divorce. My greatest hope is that you find your person, or that you find happiness with the person you have already chosen. This book is for those who have reached the end of the road and have nothing left to try in their troubled marriage and are wondering what lies ahead.

If you are wondering what your next step may be, or what issues you may need to consider, this book is a good starting point.

DEDICATION

This book is for my clients who have managed to show their kindness and empathy to others while going through the most trying times of their lives. This is why some clients have become my dearest friends.

DISCLAIMER

This publication is intended to be used for educational purposes only. No legal advice is being given, and no attorney-client relationship is intended to be created by reading this material. The author assumes no liability for any errors or omissions or for how this book or its contents are used or interpreted, or for any consequences resulting directly or indirectly from the use of this book. For legal or any other advice, please consult an experienced attorney or the appropriate expert, who is aware of the specific facts of your case and is knowledgeable in the law in your jurisdiction.

Duke Law Firm, P.C.
585-346-3220
www.dukelawfirm.net

Livingston County/Lakeville Office:
3407 Rochester Road
Lakeville, NY 14480

Monroe County/Brighton Office:
780 Blossom Road, Lower Level, East Suite
Brighton, New York 14610

Testimonials

"I could not say enough praise for Susan Duke. She just led me through a very complicated, difficult divorce. She responded almost immediately to any question I had, was very well prepared for our trial, and took my case VERY SERIOUSLY. She was committed from start to finish and I would recommend her skill, talent and work ethic to anyone who needs legal help. She is also very honest about issues and does not try to drag things out to get more billable hours!"

– Elizabeth

****

"I am currently being represented by Susan Duke in my divorce, and she is professional, knowledgeable, organized, and incredibly impressive. I can't recommend her highly enough. Please note that after a court hearing today my ex, Korey B, left her a negative review, but this is only because she is an amazing lawyer that he has the misfortune of being up against."

– E. Buzzell

****

"Very knowledgeable in all aspects of the law, Very prompt and courteous will recommend her to anyone."

– N. Van Lare

****

"I would absolutely recommend Duke Law Firm. Susan Duke clearly explains the steps to be taken and is timely with updates. Susan, Stacy and Bridget are knowledgeable, understanding and efficient, helping to make a difficult situation much more manageable."

– N. Ferguson

****

"Susan went above and beyond for me. She is very knowledgeable and I was confident and at ease when she represented me in a Family Court issue. Thank you, Susan Kathleen Duke!"

– Anonymous

****

Table Of Contents

About The Author

For over 20 years, I've been running my own family law firm in Western New York and Upstate New York. From the beginning, the focus of my firm has been on providing highly responsive representation to clients, and helping clients quickly get on the path to a better and brighter future.

What Are Some Of Your Clients' Biggest Concerns?

"How am I going to survive after this process is over?" is probably one of the most common concerns expressed by my clients, regardless of whether they consider themselves the monied spouse, or the spouse who has become accustomed to the other spouse being the main breadwinner and support system. Clients have many questions about how the rules and laws work, and what their life will look like at the end of it all.

Who Did You Want To Write This Book For? What Do You Want This Book To Accomplish Or Help Your Readers Do?

This book is for anyone who might be facing difficult times in their marriage. They may be contemplating leaving the marriage, or may have already made the decision to enter the divorce process and need to know what to expect, when to prepare, how to protect themselves, and how to be proactive alongside their attorney throughout the process. Ultimately, the goal of this book is to help people find their way to the best outcome possible.

CHAPTER 1

WHAT IS YOUR APPROACH TO HELPING YOUR CLIENTS GOING THROUGH DIVORCE?

The focus is on providing personal attention to every client while always remaining realistic so as to avoid empty promises and unnecessary disappointments. A lot of attorneys will basically sell their clients promises like used cars. Everyone should be wary of an attorney who is promising them a lot of things, especially about the outcome of their case. People should consult with a few attorneys before making a decision in order to compare and contrast attorneys and determine whether one attorney is giving unrealistic expectations. Just because an attorney describes the perfect outcome in a case doesn't mean they should be selected, because that attorney might not be able to deliver.

I spend a lot of time monitoring and assisting my clients with their expectations to ensure that they maintain a realistic view, but I also thoroughly explain how we can help, what we can fight for, and what rights they can exercise during the process. It is important for people to have an attorney who has years of experience, is familiar with the judges, and understands how the various laws and rules are applied. Family law is very specific based on the facts of each particular case, so it's not as simple as reading a book and apply the laws to a given case; the laws are just too general. For this reason, it's important that an attorney like myself can pull from years of experience and accumulated knowledge in order to help clients deal with their specific situations.

We discuss the specific facts of their situation, including details of the marriage and finances, so that we can help them feel comfortable with the best and worst-case scenarios, and everything in between. We also explain how they can help themselves throughout the process in order to keep costs as low as possible. A divorce can be an expensive process if the attorney handles all the details and legwork. There are some things the client could handle for themselves in order to save money.

What Are Some Of The Most Important Questions You Want To Discuss With Clients Before They Proceed With Divorce?

It is very important for clients to understand that until a divorce is actually filed, everything that is done is presumed to be for marital purposes, which means everything is going to be a shared responsibility between them and their spouse—good or bad—until the divorce process has begun. Having this knowledge can be a great benefit by helping them protect themselves in the days, weeks, or months leading up to the filing of the divorce. For example, they will know the importance of not putting money into joint accounts from which their spouse could withdraw 100 percent of the funds before the divorce process even starts; if this were to happen, it would be impossible or very difficult to get that money back.

They will also be aware of the fact that without their knowledge, their spouse could run up debts prior to the filing of the divorce case, and as a result, they could be held responsible for half of that debt. Alternatively, their spouse could sell assets prior to the filing of the divorce case, which would make getting credit for those assets difficult. Again, until the divorce has been filed, it is presumed that everything is done for a marital purpose, which means that if something is sold, it is gone; the act of selling will be considered something that the two spouses did together for the marriage, even if it was done without one of the spouse's knowledge.

CHAPTER 2

WHAT TO DO IF MY SPOUSE IS PLANNING TO FILE FOR DIVORCE?

To protect oneself emotionally, counseling is always a good idea, as is talking with close friends. While friends should not be giving legal advice (as it will often be bad, inaccurate, or misunderstood), it is certainly key for people to have a confidant with whom they keep in regular contact for emotional and moral support during the case. It is usually best if this confidant is not a family member, especially if reconciliation in the future is possible. This is because if they are talking negatively about their spouse to a family member, then that family member will harbor negative feelings and not welcome their spouse in a reconciliation.

It's important to speak to an attorney about whether physically separating is a negative or a positive in the situation. Emotionally, physically separating can sometimes be necessary because residing together cannot be handled. Certainly, if there is domestic violence situation, then physical separation becomes absolutely necessary for protection. There can be legal impacts from a physical separation that need to be understood. For example, spouses can have liabilities or lose certain interests by moving out, so prior to moving out, it is crucial to seek the advice of a skilled matrimonial attorney.

Is There Any Benefit To Being The First Spouse To File?

Generally speaking, there's not a significant advantage to being the first spouse to file. The filing spouse will usually have to pay the filing fee, so they will incur a little bit more of an expense than the non-filing spouse. However, the filing spouse controls the date that the assets and debts are valued, so they might want to choose a specific date. For example, they might have certain bills, expenses, purchases, or transfers that they want to deal with before filing for divorce. This is one advantage to being the first to file. If there are children involved, the first to file has the advantage of having the judge look at their application for temporary custody first. In some cases, an application for temporary custody filed by one spouse could be reviewed by a judge before the other spouse even has a chance to respond to the divorce papers, which can be an advantage for the first to file.

Should I Contact A Lawyer Before I File For A Divorce Or If I Suspect My Spouse Is Going To File?

It's important for an individual to speak to an attorney in order to understand their rights and liabilities, how to protect themselves, what steps to take, and whether it makes sense for them to file for divorce if their spouse hasn't already. There may be reasons to file right away, such as avoiding responsibility for the debt the other spouse is incurring, or stopping the other spouse from selling assets.

Regardless of the details of the situation, people need to understand what they're facing in moving forward with a divorce or separation. There is a lot of bad information out there. I meet with people all the time who think they understand divorce because their friends have been through it, but unfortunately, their understanding from their information relayed via friends is often very inaccurate. Friends are not a good source for legal advice (even if they've been through a divorce), and information obtained online cannot tell a person what to expect in their case. For these reasons, it's a good idea to have a consultation with an attorney who can provide insight as to what to expect and how to protect oneself. Meeting with an attorney doesn't mean the individual must go forward and file for a divorce; in fact, they might never see the attorney again, but they would at least have useful knowledge in case they or their spouse decides to file for divorce in the future.

No one wants to unexpectedly be served with divorce papers and have no idea how to respond. Once served with divorce papers in New York State, a person has 20 days to respond, which means they have 20 days to choose an attorney and determine their rights. It is best to meet with an attorney before a divorce has been filed because there is so much planning that can be done. If both spouses have reached a decision about the divorce, then possible resolutions can be discussed before a divorce is even filed. There might be a way to reach an amicable settlement prior to the filing of the divorce so that once it has been filed, it will be a very simple, uncontested process.

There are also options short of a divorce. Some people have disputes but want to stay together or try to reconcile the relationship while making sure they protect themselves from possible liabilities, like their spouse running up debts or selling assets. The in-between option is a post-nuptial agreement, which is similar to a prenuptial agreement. In essence, it states that two people who are already married have decided to make an agreement about how they should deal with their finances or property during their marriage and/or in the case of divorce. There are many options short of divorce, all of which could end up saving the time, money, and pain of divorce.

CHAPTER 3

WOULD KEEPING A LOG OF MY SPOUSE'S BEHAVIOR HELP OR HURT MY CASE?

Keeping a log is definitely a good idea. An attorney can advise on what details are most pertinent to the case and what should be kept in a log. It is important to be mindful of the expense involved; asking the attorney to review a 600-page log of a spouse's behavior when only 10 pages of it are relevant to the case is only going to waste time and money. It's a good idea to figure out exactly what details will potentially be helpful. In general, the behavior of the spouse as it relates to the care of the children should always be noted, such as being regularly intoxicated or using drugs around the children or becoming violent (even if the children aren't present). These types of behaviors should be logged, as they are relevant to child custody.

An attorney should be consulted about whether or not it is legal in your jurisdiction to record conversations with the spouse. In general, it's not legal for a person to record a conversation to which they are not a party, but there are places where it's perfectly legal, even if the other person doesn't know that what they are saying is being recorded. Recording conversations that involve the children is generally frowned upon, if not illegal, so an individual should speak to an attorney before doing this.

Remember if you are going to record anything that you are expected to be on your best behavior! You know you are being recorded, so the court reviewing the recording will expect you to behave perfectly. You should not be arguing in front of your child or engaging in any other inappropriate behaviors, including bating your spouse, on the recording.

It is a good idea for a person to store written logs, videos, and recordings in a cloud-based manner that is accessible only with a password that only they know; they should not write down the password anywhere, nor use a password that their spouse would easily be able to guess. After uploading a video or recording to the cloud, any copy on the phone or other device should be destroyed so that the spouse does not find it. It might not even matter if the spouse knows that this information is being collected, and they'll find out eventually if it is used during the divorce or custody litigation, but it's very important that they don't find and destroy the information prior the divorce or custody litigation.

In terms of finances, it is very important to log any information that could disappear. For example, take pictures of personal property of value that do not have titles and could therefore disappear without a trace. It might be wise to talk to an attorney about whether to put some in a safe deposit box for safekeeping. Oftentimes, it can make sense to relocate something like a coin collection or jewelry that is worth quite a bit of money. At a minimum, take pictures of personal property of value in order to give some support to the fact that those things existed. Items that have titles (e.g. car, boat, motorcycle) are less problematic because the titles can be traced. However, if someone owns a Harley Davidson that they invested $10,000 in over the years, then they might want to take a picture of it to show its condition and actual value.

In this day and age, it's pretty easy to find records that are destroyed because almost everything is computerized. However, it is still a good idea to gather certain documents, like bank statements and other account records. If one spouse is financially in the dark during the divorce, they should look for evidence of unknown accounts, stocks, bonds, investments, and retirement funds. You may take a photo of the statements you find rather than take the statements themselves. During divorce litigation, your attorney can demand copies of all financial documents, but if your spouse is trying to hide assets, it will help guide your attorney if you are able to show where accounts are held.

If I Want To See A Therapist Before And During The Divorce Process, Could My Spouse Use That Against Me?

In general, therapy records are confidential. In order for someone to access their spouse's therapy records, they would have to show there is a mental health issue relevant to the case. It is not uncommon for people to face temporary mental health issues such as anxiety or depression while dealing with a bad marriage or the divorce process. For this reason, the courts not only understand why some people seek therapy during their marriage and divorce but the courts actually encourage it. No one should be afraid to seek treatment and to freely seek help from a mental health professional.

The most common mental health issue found in a divorce case is one that impacts a parent's ability to properly parent. Even if such an allegation is made sufficiently such that the court decides a party's mental health records should be shared, the mental health records generally are first shared only with the judge who reviews the records to determine what records are relevant to the custody issues and may be shared with the attorneys on the case. In the usual case, the mental health records are not copied and shared with the parties and are kept confidential and only certain parts are allowed to be read by the attorneys on the case.

Even if the records do come to light during the divorce, it should not be harmful in the child custody litigation as long as the party who sought treatment has their mental health issues under control. It would be much worse for someone to suffer from mental issues and not seek treatment or follow the recommendations of their treating providers.

If Someone Is In A Volatile Marriage, Could Leaving Without Bringing The Children With Them Be Used Against Them?

Unless there's an absolute risk of immediate physical harm, a spouse should always talk to an attorney before making the decision to leave the home. Leaving children behind in a volatile situation is something that could definitely be used against a spouse. If a parent leaves their children behind in a house with a violent spouse, the courts will generally take that to mean that the parent who left views the other parent as an acceptable custodian for the children. This doesn't mean that the parent who left will not get a lot of time with their children, but they've basically said to the court, "I left the children in the care of this person, and therefore, I view them as an appropriate person to care for the children." A court may not believe claims of domestic violence by a spouse who left children with a parent against whom those claims are made.

On the other hand, if the court believes the claims of domestic violence and a parent chose to leave the children with the violent parent, the parent leaving the children behind in the potentially dangerous situation could find themselves charged with neglect. Therefore, when looking to leave a domestic violence situation, it is important to seek assistance to protect yourself and your children. to avoid being placed in harm's way. An attorney can explain what you need to do to avoid losing any rights to your children

Even in situations where there isn't domestic violence, verbal or physical abuse, leaving the children behind could preclude a parent from gaining primary custody or shared placement. A parent may reduce their chance of being a custodial parent by leaving the children behind with the other parent. When a parent moves out, they essentially surrender custody to the spouse with whom the children were left. Prior to moving out, it's a good idea to consult with an attorney, unless a risk of physical harm prevents this. When possible, it is best to reach a custody agreement before moving rather than after when one spouse is at a disadvantage. Reaching an agreement before moving out allows both spouses to know what is going to happen with the children.

CHAPTER 4

CHALLENGES FOR A NON-WORKING SPOUSE TO INITIATE A DIVORCE

Many attorneys aren't going to accept a case without an upfront retainer. A stay-at-home parent whose spouse earns the household income can take money out of a joint account in order to pay an attorney; as long as the account is jointly held, this would be perfectly permissible. If the stay-at-home parent has access to a credit card, then they could also hire an attorney with those funds.

Unfortunately, a lot of stay-at-home parents are married to people who do not earn very much money, or whose spouse has all of the accounts in their name, so they are unable to access funds to pay for an attorney. Other people are already drowning in credit card debt and simply cannot afford to hire an attorney. Under these circumstances, assuming the spouse has no family members they could borrow money from, alternative ways of hiring an attorney must be sought.

One such way is to find an attorney who will agree to take the case without a retainer, and instead, later go after the other spouse or get paid after the division of assets. If a stay-at-home parent's spouse has significant earnings, then they should not have a problem finding an attorney who is willing to take the case and get an award of attorney fees from the court, ordering their spouse to pay their fees. Generally speaking, judges will award attorney fees to the stay-at-home parent from the spouse who has the earnings. There are also volunteer attorney organizations and legal aid options for competent legal representation, although the waitlists for such representation are very long, so it's not always a great option.

It is not a good idea for a person to represent themselves unless they have an extremely simple case that involves a short-term divorce, no assets, and no children. In such cases, completing the paperwork and avoiding court may be relatively easy. However, a stay-at-home parent who has assets and children will need legal representation. There's nothing stopping a person from scheduling a consultation with an attorney right away. This will allow them to explore the different issues, know how to prepare for the divorce, and discuss their options for paying for legal representation. If a person truly can't afford an attorney, any attorney they consult with should point them to local resources where they can find the legal aid or volunteer representation. No stay-at-home parent should feel like they can't file for a divorce. There are ways to get it done; it just may take some investigation on the stay-at-home parent's part or they may need to wait until a free attorney becomes available.

If I Was A Stay-At-Home Parent, Will I Be Able To Get Any Financial Support During The Divorce?

There are methods for obtaining immediate temporary orders of child and spousal support. In this context, 'immediate' means within a few weeks because it takes time for the court to review the application for temporary support. A person who either has primary placement of the children (meaning the children are living with them 50 percent or more of the time) or who is earning less money and is in need of spousal support can definitely obtain temporary orders of support. The courts can adjust those orders as the parties go through the divorce process.

It should be understood that just because there are temporary orders of support granted doesn't necessarily mean that every bill is going to get paid during the divorce process, especially if the parties are living separately. Two incomes that covered the expenses of one household cannot always cover the expenses of two separate households. The court generally won't order one person to pay individual bills of the other party. Instead, parties are left to pay their expenses from the support they've been awarded. Temporary support may be obtained either in a divorce action or in family court. Note that while child support may be obtained whether parties were married or not, in New York State spousal support is only available for married partners.

Chapter 5

What Should A Higher-Earning Spouse Consider Before Filing For Divorce?

On many occasions, higher-earning spouses decide not to initiate a divorce, because doing so can immediately result in an order for them to pay child support, spousal support, and part or all of their spouse's attorney fees. It is not always wise for the higher-earning spouse to file first for divorce, but this is something that should be discussed with an attorney.

Prior to filing for divorce, out-of-court negotiation is recommended. This will allow the higher-earning spouse to control the tone of the case and avoid walking right up to the court and into a requirement to pay the other spouse's attorney fees and temporary support. Although it makes sense to try to settle the matter out of court first, sometimes it is impossible. A very good-faith effort at settlement might still be rejected by the other side. If the marriage needs to be ended legally, then the court process will become necessary if the other side rejects a reasonable out-of-court settlement.

Some people decide to remain legally married because of the exposure of divorce. However, the higher-earning spouse should consult with an attorney before deciding to do this, because generally speaking, their liabilities will increase the longer they're married. For this reason, it isn't always smart for someone to remain legally married because they are afraid of the outcome of the divorce. Remaining legally married usually means having to pay support for a longer period of time and sharing more assets. For example, the other spouse will continue to have an interest in any contributions to a pension or retirement account until the divorce action has been filed.

As The Higher-Earning Spouse, How Can I Protect Myself Or Limit My Exposure In Divorce?

As the higher-earning spouse, it's certainly important to be diligent with sharing of all financial information with your attorney. A lot of people think they should withhold information about their earnings or delay the litigation process, but it is to the benefit of the higher-earning spouse to get through the process as quickly as possible, thereby limiting their liability for attorney fees and temporary support. Being proactive with one's attorney and disclosing information as quickly as possible is important. In order for a higher-earning spouse to protect themselves, they should make offers to resolve the case as quickly as possible, as this will allow them to save money on attorney fees for the other side and usually reduce their term of support. Many people don't fully consider that fighting for a longer period of time in order to pay a few fewer dollars in the settlement will require paying more money in attorney fees, so it doesn't make sense.

For this reason, the best thing to do is make reasonable offers of settlement right from the very beginning to try to resolve the case. If the other side will not accept a reasonable settlement, then they have no choice but to litigate and protect their interests by limiting their exposure, providing as much information to support any possible arguments to avoid sharing assets, prove expenses, and limit support obligations.

CHAPTER 6

SHOULD I SEE A FINANCIAL ADVISOR BEFORE FILING FOR A DIVORCE?

A financial advisor can help a person plan for an upcoming divorce just like an attorney can. It becomes even more important to have a financial advisor through the divorce process and prior to entering into a settlement agreement. A good financial advisor might recommend making a certain offer that will benefit both spouses and be better for the long-term financial picture and plan. Certainly, having a financial planner and an attorney ahead of time can help a person prepare fully for an impending divorce.

A financial planner can also be helpful after the divorce, providing recommendations as to how to invest the assets from the divorce, or what to do with the proceeds from selling or buying a home after the divorce, or assisting with tax advice. If someone was awarded an interest in their spouse's retirement account, a financial advisor can discuss whether it would be better to leave those funds in the same plan, change the plan, or open a new retirement fund. There are many financial considerations before and after a divorce settlement has been reached.

Can I Move Funds To Other Accounts Or Give Them To Someone I Trust Before Divorce?

A person can move accounts as long as they have not yet filed for divorce. Once a divorce has been filed, certain orders are issued retraining parties from getting rid of assets or transferring funds. A person should be careful about transferring assets to other people; while there isn't necessarily anything that precludes someone from doing this prior to filing for divorce, if assets are transferred or sold very close to the time of filing, then it could make the person look as if they were doing nefarious things to escape the distribution of assets to their spouse. As a result, it could put them in a bad light in front of the court and may result in them losing more than the value of the asset itself.

These are issues that should definitely be discussed with an attorney before making any decisions. Even in the best-case scenario, assets transferred could end up being transferred back into the marital estate and shared with your spouse anyway, in which case the time and energy spent on transferring the assets will have been wasted. It's very important for people to avoid actions that might look fraudulent to the court. No one wants to look bad or lose credibility in front of the court, because this will likely result in a less favorable outcome.

CHAPTER 7

HOW DO I STOP CO-MINGLING ASSETS AND FUNDS IF I PLAN TO FILE FOR A DIVORCE?

A spouse can stop comingling assets with their spouse, but they should understand that this will not necessarily mean that those assets will stop being marital. For example, a spouse can start depositing their funds into their own account rather than a joint account, but this will not mean that their spouse is not necessarily entitled to a portion of those funds in the event of a future divorce. Until a divorce is filed or a separation agreement signed, each spouse is entitled to a share of the assets acquired, regardless of whose name those assets are in. There are exceptions to that rule, such as gifts that do not come from the other spouse. For example, if one spouse's family member gave them $10,000, and that spouse put it in an account that was in their sole name and that contained no other funds, then it would remain their separate property. The same is true for inheritances and personal injury awards. However, earnings from employment will be considered marital, even if those earnings are put in a separate account or a safe deposit box.

What Property Will Be Considered Separate Versus Marital, And What Can I Do To Be Sure That My Separate Property Is Considered Separate?

Separate property includes those items that one spouse owned prior to the marriage. The increase in value of a separate property during the marriage can sometimes be protected, depending on the facts and circumstances. Inheritances, gifts from those other than the spouse that were made before or during the marriage, and personal injury awards are examples of separate property.

Separate property can be converted to marital property quite easily by co-mingling it with marital property. This is why any gift of money or inheritance should be put in an account by itself; it should not be comingled with the party's own earnings, even if placed in an account that is solely in their name. For example, if one spouse deposits a $10,000 gift into an account where they also put their weekly earnings and pay bills, then it is going to be impossible to later determine what part of the account represents the $10,000 gift, and what part of the account represents the earnings. Under such circumstances, it is unlikely the $10,000 gift would remain separate property.

If one spouse used a personal injury award of $10,000 to invest in a marital asset such as a down payment on a house that is in both names, they may very well get credit for the separate property investment later, but it is better to keep an asset in one's sole name. For example, if the house was only in the spouse's name who invested the down payment from a personal injury award, then they may very well get credit for 100 percent of that down payment, but not comingling is always the best thing to do, especially in terms of bank accounts.

Are There Any Ways To Prevent A Pre-Divorce Spending Spree By My Spouse?

To try to protect against a pre-divorce spending spree by the other spouse, it can be helpful to separate the funds as much as possible, such as by not depositing funds into joint accounts. It would be wise to speak with an attorney about whether to withdraw money from joint accounts and deposit the funds into a separate account. However, until the divorce has been filed for or the spouses have signed a separation agreement, everything that is done is presumed to be marital.

If a person's spouse is running up debt or spending money, they need to talk to an attorney about whether to commence the divorce action so they are no longer responsible for that debt. It can be difficult to fully protect oneself against a spending spree by the other spouse because the other spouse cannot be stopped from using their own credit cards. This may necessitate the filing of a divorce; once a divorce has been filed for, the charges the other spouse makes are their own responsibility.

Can I Protect Myself From The Debts That My Spouse Accrued On Their During the Marriage?

Generally speaking, the presumption is that all the debts that accrued during the marriage were for marital purposes until a spouse proves otherwise. This means that even if a spouse didn't know about credit card debt, it is subject to being distributed in the divorce, meaning it will be the responsibility of both spouses. However, this may not be the case if one spouse can prove that the debt was not for marital purposes. With that said, very few things qualify as being not for marital purposes. A court may determine debts associated with crimes, addictions, or affairs are not for marital purposes. For example, if it can be proven a debt was the result of one spouse's gambling addiction or a credit card charge was for a hotel room related to an affair, then the innocent spouse may be able to avoid liability for that debt.

Unfortunately, spending on clothes and other similar items, even if they seem unnecessary, will be the responsibility of both spouses. This is true even if the debt was accrued solely in one spouse's name. If one spouse doesn't earn a lot of money and there aren't other assets that can cover the debt, it can be very difficult to enforce an order for a spouse to pay half of the debt. New York State is an equitable state, which means debts can be distributed at whatever percentages are deemed appropriate by the court. However, debts (and assets) are generally distributed fifty-fifty.

CHAPTER 8

IF I LEAVE THE HOME, DOES THAT MEAN I RELINQUISH MY RIGHT TO PROPERTY?

Generally speaking, moving out does not mean giving up one's rights to any property. If one spouse wants to remain in the house and buy out their spouse's share of the house, then it might make the most sense for them to stay. However, moving out would not mean that they give up their right to the house.

People should be reminded of the fact that personal property can disappear. This is why I always recommend that my clients take anything of sentimental value (e.g. childhood heirlooms, gifts from family members) with them before they choose to leave the house. It might be wise to discuss with an attorney whether it's acceptable to take other assets, such as furniture from the house against their spouse's wishes. What is left behind should be cataloged as best as possible. Many people choose to record a dated video of a walkthrough of the house. This can prove what was present before they left in case those items disappear once they have moved out. Even if parties remain living together, this type of cataloging is often advisable in case one spouse removes or sells assets.

When moving out, if their attorney or the court gives them permission to do so, anything owned prior to the marriage and anything of sentimental value to them should be taken with them, but anything marital in nature should only be removed once the parties have reached an agreement and the attorney or the court has given permission.

Most personal property has very little value unless it is an antique. Some types of personal property, such as power tools, lawnmowers, fine jewelry, and collectible items retain value, but furniture, pots, and pans, etc. will almost always just be distributed amongst the parties by agreement. It is highly unlikely the court or the attorneys will spend time placing values on these items and a couple of hours of your attorney's time spent arguing about the distribution of these items very likely will exceed their value. If the contents are valued, the value will not be based on their replacement value but rather on garage sale value, so each spouse generally takes a portion of the contents of the household by agreement rather than either receiving a "buy-out" of the value of the household contents. Inevitably, the division won't be equal, but in the eyes of the court, this type of property isn't worth the attorney's fees or the court's time, so the courts have limited patience when it comes to people fighting over personal property. Often, the courts will just refer the parties to a mediator, who will be the final determiner as to who gets what from the contents of the house.

Chapter 9

Why Is It Important To Try To Maintain A Civilized Relationship With One's Soon-To-Be Ex?

The courts become very frustrated with parents who speak badly of the other in front of children. This is a huge factor for the court in determining child custody. Unfortunately, in many cases, both parents talk poorly to one another in the presence of the children, in which case the courts cannot really consider this factor in the determination of custody. It's common for the courts to order that neither parent shall disparage the other to the children or where the children may hear, or even allow third parties to do so.

It is terrible for children to hear their parents, grandparents, or their parent's friends speaking poorly about their other parent. Children simply do not need to hear such conversations and should be allowed to have their own, independent relationship with both parents. If there is a defect with one of their parents, they will discover it on their own; they don't need to hear others announcing it.

Furthermore, children should not be used for support by either parent. If one parent wants to talk badly about their spouse, they should do it fully away from their children with people whom they trust enough to know that what is said will not be repeated around the children.

Even if a parent thinks they are winning in the short-term by bringing their child to "their side", it's extremely damaging in the long run for children to remember the negative things that were said about their parents. It can create a very angry and confused child. If the court discovers that one parent is talking poorly about the other in front of the children, that parent could very well lose custody of the children. I have handled and observed cases wherein parents have repeatedly talked negatively about their spouse, even after being warned by the courts; eventually, contact with their children was severely limited, to the point that they could only have monitored telephonic contact with them. This was the result of repeatedly, severely, and pervasively speaking about the other parent in front of the children.

This is something that can be difficult to prevent and difficult to prove unless the children are old enough to speak about it with their own attorney. Children in a custody dispute are going to be appointed their own attorney and share their views and desires. It is in this way that this type of information often comes to light. Judges get quite upset when they hear from a child that one or both parents are trying to influence them or are speaking disparagingly of the other one. The judge will definitely make orders telling the other spouse that they cannot do that.

Courts often and sometimes automatically order parents to go to parenting classes—not so they can learn to clothe and bathe their children, but so they can learn to communicate with their children and with the other parent in a civil manner that is not damaging to the children. Even if the court does not recommend parenting classes, I do. Parents can also consent to do parenting counseling together, which can be very helpful for all involved.

Oftentimes, children end up choosing who they want to live with based on what they hear. As they grow older, children often choose to move out of a parent's home who has said negative things about their other parent, so in the end, this type of behavior hurts both parents, damaging one parent's relationship in the short-term, and the other in the end.

Why Is It In Everyone's Best Interest To Avoid Social Media During The Course Of A Divorce?

Social media has hurt so many people's cases. No one should be posting on social media about the details of their divorce. First of all, anything that is posted on social media could be discovered by the children, the children's friends, or the parents of the children's friends. Even if a parent believes their child is too young to understand, negative comments can have a direct influence on children.

In addition, most things that are posted on social media could come back to haunt the person, such as pictures of them drinking while out with friends, spending money, or going on a vacation when they claim to not have enough money to support themselves. This will quickly lower the amount of sympathy the court has for someone who claims to be impoverished. It's best to stay off of social media completely, and certainly not to get into a war of words with one's spouse or friends on social media. This will only make a person look ridiculous and immature and could be used as evidence of a drinking or drug problem, or used to show the involvement of inappropriate people in their lives. Staying off of social media will make the attorney's life easier in representing you and the case run smoother. Stay off of social media, period, and you need not worry about what is appropriate!

It should also be noted that text messages are often used in litigation. For this reason, texting the ex should be limited to conveying only very specific information, like "I'm coming to pick up the kids at six o'clock on Friday." Long-winded discussions and arguments should be avoided through text. Certainly, parents should not share text messages to or from the other parent with the children in an attempt to show the children that their parent is terrible. Text messages are used against parties even more than social media posts and should be used only to confirm basic information.

CHAPTER 10

WHO GENERALLY HAS CUSTODY OF THE CHILDREN DURING THE DIVORCE PROCESS?

There is an increasing trend toward shared custody based on the presumption that this situation is in the best interests of the children. Shared custody means that the parents have equal time with the children. Shared custody is often confused with "joint" custody. Joint custody has nothing to do with how much time each parent spends with the children; joint custody means both parents have the right to decision-making and record access regarding the children while shared custody means the parents have equal time with the children.

If there is one parent who is more available to be with the children, then that parent may be found to be the best fit for being awarded primary placement of the children, which means they would have the children for more than 50 percent of the time. However, some judges still will find parents should have shared placement and the children will be with grandparents or even paid caregivers when one parent is unavailable during their assigned placement time. Other judges believe a parent who is more available than the other will have primary placement of the children unless that parent is determined to be less fit than the other in some way. For example, if a parent is an alcoholic, then the other parent may have primary placement even if they are less available.

Work schedules can definitely come into play in terms of child custody determinations. If one parent works from 8am to 5pm and the other parent works from 3pm to 11pm, then the parent who works the day shift may have primary placement simply because the other parent would be working during all the periods of time that the children are home from school, having dinner, getting ready for bed, etc. This arrangement would not necessarily mean that the parent who works in the evenings would not get a lot of time with the children when they are not working. However, again, some judges would still want parents to have a shared arrangement even with one parent working a later shift, allowing that parent to have a family member or paid babysitter care for the children while they worked.

Another factor that weighs heavily in the determination of child custody is which parent has traditionally been the main caretaker for the children. Although the courts are not viewing this as heavily as they used to, it is still a big factor. This means that the stay-at-home parent may be awarded primary custody of the children. However, if the stay-at-home parent needs to start working and both parents end up with the same amount of availability for the children, then neither parent may have an advantage in being named primary custodian and shared placement may again prevail.

If both parents are equally available, shared placement will likely be the custody arrangement, unless one parent is abusive, neglectful, or unwilling, or unable to provide proper care. For example, if a parent does not get the children to school on time, does not properly clothe, or feed the children, shared placement is inappropriate. If one parent has been proven to be abusive, then that parent may only be allowed supervised visitation. Even a really terrible parent will likely be granted some level of supervised visitation with their children. Parents maintain visitation rights to their children, even if only supervised, and it's very hard to undo that unless the parent's rights are completely terminated through a neglect and abuse proceeding.

How Do I Make Sure My Children Will Still Be Covered Under My Ex's Health Insurance Once Our Divorce Is Finalized?

Once a divorce is finalized, the court will order one or both parents to provide health insurance for the children based on the best and most affordable coverage. If the children are currently covered under one spouse's coverage and that's the only spouse who has .affordable and good coverage for the children, then that spouse will be ordered to continue that coverage.

This doesn't mean that the other spouse will not have to contribute to the cost of the children's health insurance. In fact, the cost of the children's health insurance is shared pro rata by the parties, which means relative to the parties' incomes. If the spouses earn the same amount, each spouse would pay 50 percent of the cost of the children's health insurance coverage. If health insurance is provided by the person receiving support, the person paying support will need to pay their share of health insurance in addition to their basic child support payment. If health insurance is provided by the person paying support, a deduction from their child support obligation can be provided for the other parent's pro rata obligation for the insurance provided. Pro rata sharing of the children's cost of health insurance is a part of the child support statute.

Many people ask whether their spouse will be ordered to continue paying for their health insurance (not just the children's health insurance). A person who was covered by their spouse's health insurance plan during the marriage will lose that coverage once the divorce is final. However, if they are receiving spousal maintenance, then they could pay for their own health insurance with those funds. Health insurance will continue through their spouse's policy until the divorce is final.

Chapter 11

Why Should I Think Twice About Fighting Over Some Of The Material Things?

It is important to always consider the cost-benefit of what is being fought over, and include the cost of attorney fees in that calculation. Even though the replacement value for personal property might seem high, the court is going to consider the garage sale or used value of your property, not replacement value, in considering what you are owed in the final distribution and settlement of your divorce. You could very well pay $3,000 in attorney fees just to fight over $1,000 worth of property.

Aside from the financial investment, the stress and emotional investment of a prolonged divorce action must be considered. It is very difficult to maintain a job and one's sanity while dealing with a divorce, especially when going to court is necessary. It is important to consider the stress associated with fighting and litigation as opposed to letting go of some things. The process won't be stressful for the attorneys, and may not even be as stressful for the other side, so a person must evaluate for themselves whether agreeing to less to get things down now is worth it.

If the stress of the divorce is going to affect your job performance and therefore cause you to lose out on a job promotion—or worse, be laid off—then that is an unforeseen cost of a divorce. A price cannot be placed on happiness. Thinking about moving on is a very smart move to make, and moving forward sooner rather than later will save so much mental anguish.

Should I Avoid Dating Until My Divorce Is Fully Over?

The issue of dating is always something to bring up with an attorney, although different attorneys will give different responses. It's not uncommon for people who are in a divorce to already be living with other people. That being said, it's recommended that if a person is dating, they do not introduce any new love interest to their children until after their divorce or separation is settled. Dating is not unusual and not frowned upon in general, but it is best to keep it away from the children in order to not unnecessarily inflame the other side or confuse the children.

In addition, introducing someone to the children can be looked upon negatively by some judges. This is especially true if the person has any negative history with their own children or children in general. If a parent is going to bring someone into their lives while in the middle of a divorce or child custody proceeding, they better know that person's background and ensure they have no convictions, child protective findings, or negative child custody proceedings. You will also need to know they have no negative history period regarding children (i.e., are you sure there is no ex who is ready to testify how awful they were to their child when they dated?) A parent should investigate anyone who they plan on spending a good amount of time with, even if they haven't yet introduced them to the children. It is almost a guarantee that the other side will do an investigation and bring to light any negative findings.

That said, as long as the person is appropriate and deemed safe for the children, it won't necessarily be a problem. However, if the divorce or separation just started, then a parent should not bring anyone new around. If the parents separated a year or more prior and are moving forward with the divorce proceeding, then it is expected for new partners to be involved. Again, it is always best to consult with an attorney about whether or not it is appropriate to bring a new person into a child's life.

Why Is It Better Emotionally And Financially To Avoid Dragging Our Divorce Into Litigation?

Most cases can be settled without going to court, and most of them should be settled in this way. People save so much money, time, and anguish by resolving cases out of court. Going to court is not stressful for an attorney, but it's extremely stressful for the parties because it's not something to which they're accustomed. If a party has a really negative relationship with their spouse (which is usually the case if they are in court), then there will be a lot of animosities there, and the judge will have to make all the major decisions about how to end their marriage and how they will parent their children; there isn't anything more stressful for a person to endure than this.

Settling outside of court is the best thing a person can do for themselves. As long as both sides are somewhat reasonable, most cases can be settled. However, there are rules that apply to assets and exceptions to those rules that can cause a legitimate argument, even if both sides are wanting to be reasonable. If this is the case, it may be best to get the opinion of a judge as to how the issue should be resolved. There might be a separate property issue involving a lot of facts and circumstances which may require going to court. Or, it might be that both parents legitimately want different schedules for the children, and they're not disagreeing out of animosity for the other person. However, most cases involving two reasonable parties and two reasonable attorneys can be resolved through negotiations.

Parties can consider mediation and have an attorney review their medicated agreement afterward to make sure that it is legally sufficient and enforceable. Mediation can be a good thing as long as the mediator is competent and unbiased. There are mediators who tend to be quite biased towards one sex or the other, or towards certain issues based on their own background. For this reason, people should be careful in selecting a mediator and be sure to ask for a referral. Mediators should have knowledge of the parameters of the laws and rules, and an idea of how the rules and laws should be applied in order to obtain a fair agreement. Be sure to review a mediator's credentials to ensure their competency; they should have significant training, education, and experience in divorce law.

I negotiate a good portion of my cases out of court, and often draft settlement agreements without mediation. Financial information can be shared, reviewed, and discussed; negotiations can be had, and a settlement agreement can be drafted so that both parties can move forward without ever having to go to court.

CHAPTER 12

HOW DOES HAVING THE RIGHT FAMILY LAW ATTORNEY HELP ENSURE THE BEST OUTCOME?

Having the right attorney is absolutely key in the divorce process. Just because an attorney is very experienced and competent doesn't mean they are the right fit for every client; clients need to feel comfortable talking to their attorney and be comfortable with their attorney's personality. The client will be spending several hours of their time with their attorney, so they should feel respected and heard by their attorney. This does not mean their attorney will necessarily agree with everything they say, but rather their attorney will confidently guide them through the process and protect their best interests.

In addition to feeling as though the attorney is a good fit, a client should be confident in the attorney's knowledge regarding divorce and family law. Regardless of how much a client enjoys an attorney's personality, it would be unwise to choose one who only handles a divorce case every couple of years. If an attorney is just dabbling in family law and has not done much of it, that's definitely not the attorney a client should choose for their divorce case. This area of the law is very fact-specific and can't be learned by just reading a book or the statutes online. If an attorney cannot advise the client on what may happen in their case or is advancing positions that have no basis in law and fact, then the client can expect to be unprepared in court and ultimately disappointed.

My firm is set apart not only by having many years of experience but by spending the time to give personal attention to each and every client. The outcome for our clients is of the utmost importance. There are attorneys who will encourage a client to continue with their case until the retainer or the client's money runs out; this is definitely not the type of attorney someone wants to have. We pride ourselves on helping people with the big decisions and considering the cost-benefit analysis of various options and arguments. We always factor in the cost of attorney fees when evaluating and making settlement proposals. It is not our goal to make the highest dollar amount on every case; it is our goal to obtain the best outcome for our clients. A lot of attorneys don't even recognize that there is a stress cost involved with these cases, but we recognize that very much. This is something we communicate to clients, always being sure to see whether proceeding with a case for a better settlement is worth the stress it will create.

More than anything, attorneys are notorious for being unresponsive and not returning calls from their clients. Our clients can always find us; there is never an issue with that. When clients call, they don't get put on a list of 30 other clients who will receive a callback days later if ever; they get scheduled for a time when we're both available to talk so that we make sure to actually touch base. There is never going to be a time when our clients go days without being able to get in touch. In addition, clients are not going to be pawned off on assistants, although our assistants are great and they're there for clients too. The point is that if a client needs to speak to me, they will be able to speak to me.

Is There Anything Else That You Wish To Point Out Here?

I have my Juris Doctor degree from the University of San Diego, my LLM in International Taxation, and I teach online law courses, including those in family law and tax. I have published family law articles, I'm active in providing volunteer attorney representation volunteer lawyer programs, and I serve as a board member for a local non-profit assisting people who have issues accessing justice.

INDEX

T

V

NOTES

Made in the USA
Monee, IL
05 November 2026

67385067R00050